Discipleship Books:

The Cross and The Triangle

One Lord, one faith.

By

Philip Watson

Discipleship Books Ministry P O Box 21731
Henderson, Auckland, New Zealand.

ISBN 978-0-473-31152-0

Dedicated to my wife Dianne

And three children,

Andrew Jonathan and Ruth

And Nicholas – a wonderful grandson

Special thanks to Warren Portsmouth, who patiently went through each manuscript with me, pointing out grammatical errors and making suggestions for improving the script. He assisted in so many other ways including designing most of the covers.

Special thanks to the Holy Spirit. Every book I have written, has been at the prompting of the Holy Spirit. Once I began writing each book, the Holy Spirit brought back to my memory, Bible verses that were relevant to each part of each book.

In bringing back to my memory relevant Bible verses, the Holy Spirit was doing what Jesus predicted he would do. John 14:26

Discipleship Books by Philip Watson

The Jesus Series:

Jesus The Ministry

Jesus The Incarnation

Jesus Changed Our Lives

The Trinity Series

The Father

The Son

The Holy Spirit

Other Books

The Cross and The Triangle

Successful Relationships

101 Spiritual Principles

1000 Great Quotes

Great Summaries

Contents

Introduction

This is one of the shorter books I have written, but   possibly the most important - because it encompasses four dimensions of the faith, and ties them all together!

1. The nature of the Father/ Son and Holy Spirit.

2. The relationship of the Father/Son and Holy Spirit to us, human beings.

3. Our relationship (as disciples of Jesus) to one another and other people.

4. Our relationship as disciples of Jesus

to the Father, the Son and Holy Spirit.

In a few words' this book covers 'every' dimension of the faith and if readers grasp what this book is really about, they will realise that:

> *What we believe and what we do, are one and the same.*

The message of this book has been staring at us from the pages of the Bible but some-how has not been identified because of the way we (that is authors, teachers/preachers and those who have written the lyrics of hymns/choruses) have treated the faith. We have divided it up into separate compartments or rooms.

Often in the Church, when authors/song writers and those who have preached sermons, have described the nature of God; it is as if they have put the nature of God in one room and the nature of Jesus in another and the nature of the Holy Spirit, in another room - as if the nature of all three, were separate and different!

Then the way the Father/Son and Holy Spirit relate to us human beings, has been treated as if it was, a separate pathway or subject.

And the Christian life, the one we live day by

day has been treated as if it were a separate pathway or subject.

Finally our relationship to the Father/Son and Holy Spirit, has been treated as if it was, a separate pathway or subject.

The message of this book is that these separate rooms containing the Father/Son/ and Holy Spirit are linked – as is the way they relate to us, the way we relate to one another and finally our relationship to the Father/Son and Holy Spirit.

These rooms and relationships are all linked by common values and there are no dividing walls between them.

Expressed in symbols, these shared values of the Father/Son and Holy Spirit and which permeate their relationship with us and our relationship to one another and our relationship to the Father/Son and Holy Spirit; are like the arms of a cross, with a triangle below it.

When I first began thinking about the message of this book and how to convey it, I thought of the flag of India which has a wheel on it. The wheel is on the Indian flag because a key belief of the Hindu faith (the majority of Indians are Hindu) is that God is everything and everything is God – and a wheel with it's many spokes that connect the hub to the outer rim of the wheel, symbolizes that God is everything, and everything is God.

We Christians have a similar world-view that everything is connected, but our starting point is not the same as the Hindu faith (where God is everything and everything is God). Our starting point is that everything was created by God but everything God created is 'separate' from God.

However, even though everything created by God, is separate from God, the nature of God 'infuses' every being in heaven, and infuses their relationship with us, if we will allow it. And infuses the relationships between humans and human relationships, with the Father, Son and Holy Spirit.

For those reasons, a cross with a triangle below it, are the most appropriate symbols to represent the message of this book.

The cross because, at the center of it, is God the Father. To one side of the cross, is Jesus his Son, and to the other side, the Holy Spirit. Then down the first side of the triangle go their shared values, eventually returning to God the Father.

We should not be surprised that the Son and Holy Spirit share exactly the same values as the Father, because as the Apostle Paul wrote.

> *"For God was pleased to have all his fullness dwell in him (Jesus) ...." Col 1:19 –*

In a few words, Paul was saying. God's complete nature and values, can be found in his Son Jesus.

We should not be surprised that the Holy Spirit, also shares the same values as God the Father. The Apostle wrote this about the Holy Spirit.

> *"We have not received the spirit of this world, but the Spirit who is from God...." 1 Cor 2: 12 NIV*

The Holy Spirit is "from God". In another translation those same words are rendered, "of God". "From God" or "of God" - it does not matter which rendering is preferred because both convey the same idea - that the Holy Spirit shares the same nature and values as, God the Father.

The second symbol on the front cover of this book, is the triangle. That symbol was selected because, those values which all three members of the trinity share, do not stop at the borders of heaven but come down the first side of the triangle to us human beings.

Then, we who are the recipients of those values, will hopefully share them with our fellow human beings, creating the second or bottom arm of the triangle. Then finally, creating the third arm of the triangle, is when we return those same values to the God Father.

I tried to find in the Bible, a single verse that captures the message of this book but could not find one that, on it's own, captures the message of this book. There are many that collectively capture the message of this book.

If there is one verse that 'largely' captures the message of this book, it is this one.

> *"For from Him (that is God) and to Him; and through Him; are all things.... " Rom 11:36 NIV*

If I had permission from the Apostle Paul to alter those words so that they capture the message of this book, that verse would read.

- *For from Him and to The Son & Holy Spirit (the arms of the cross)*

- *and to us (the first side of the*

triangle)

- and through us (the second side of the triangle)

- *and to Him* (the third side of the triangle)

- *are all things.....*

Another verse that largely captures the message of this book, is this one.

..one Lord, one faith, one baptism. One God and father of us all.

- - - - - - - -

In this Introduction, as simply as I possible, I have tried to explain the message of this book. If readers have not quite grasped that message from the introduction, it will become much clearer as you read through this book and will see, from example after example, how the same values follow the arms of the cross to the Son and Holy Spirit, and then around the three legs of the triangle.

Before you begin to read this book, you may recognize some significant sub-themes in it.

1. The nature of the trinity.

2. It is implicit in the message of this book

that we were designed and built to live in fellowship with the Father, Son and Holy Spirit. In the Bible, the word 'fellowship' is associated with all three members of the trinity. Meaning, we humans were created to have fellowship with the Father/Son and Holy Spirit. Or as someone has said, "we have a God-shaped vacuum in our lives" and if God does not fill it, people try and fill that vacuum with a variety of, poor substitutes.

3. We were designed to be vessels of the nature and values of God. That is, we were designed to be vessels of the love and truth and faith and holiness, and all the other values that are part of the nature of the Father, Son and Holy Spirit.

May God bless you as you read and understand, the message of this book.

Philip Watson

Chapter 1

Love

The Apostle John wrote, 'God is love'. 1 John 5:8 If our faith stopped there, we could say to ourselves. "That is a good, the God we worship, is love - and those who make it to heaven will, one day, experience that love.

The love of God   however, is not restricted to God the father. If we follow one arm of the cross out to Jesus, we find that he also was, and is, loving. Love was a characteristic of Jesus during his time of ministry on Earth. So it is obvious that Jesus shares the same value of love, the Father has.

But what about the Holy Spirit? If we follow the other arm of the cross out to where the Holy Spirit is; we find that the Holy Spirit also, shares that same value of love as the Father and the Son. In the book of Galatians, Paul listed the fruits of the Spirit. One of those fruits, is love. What is not often considered, is this. The Holy Spirit can only share with us, what is an integral part of his nature!

So for the Holy Spirit to share the fruit of love with us. Love must be an integral part of his nature – a nature that he received from, God the Father.

Now that the arms of the cross has been explained; we have a wonderful picture of the trinity. The Father/Son and Holy Spirit, all share the same value – love.

Side one of the triangle

However, the message of the Bible, is this. The love which the Father/Son and Holy Spirit collectively share, does not stop at the borders of heaven. They already have, and are, and will continue to share; that love, with the people of this Earth.

A verse that reiterates this,

> *"For God so loved the world that he gave his one and only Son...."* John

3:16

Another verse that reiterates that same truth,

> *"For we know how dearly God loves us, because he has given the Holy Spirit to fill our hearts with his love." Rom 5:5 NLT*

That is the first side of the divine triangle, the Father/Son and Holy Spirit, all sharing their love with those who will receive it.

Side two of the triangle

Now to the lower arm of the triangle. The love we have received, is not meant to stop with those of us who have received God's love and the love of Jesus and the love of the Holy Spirit. Jesus urged his disciples in various teachings, to share that love, with other people. When we do that, we complete, the second side of the triangle.

When Jesus was asked which commandments were the greatest, he identified two commandments. The second commandment, was a Jesus original*. He said, "Love your neighbor, as yourself." Matt 22:39

*This commandment is not found in the laws of the Old Testament but is one Jesus created.

There are many different ways, Jesus urged his disciples to share the love they had received. By forgiving others, by giving to others, by praying for others, by making loans and not expecting repayment. Jesus even urged his disciples to love their enemies and he concluded his teachings about loving our enemies, with these words.

> "Be   perfect...as   your   heavenly Father is perfect." Matt 5:48.

By those words, Jesus was saying. If you want to be like God the Father, love, even your enemies.

Side three of the triangle

Then there is the third leg of the triangle. That third leg is completed when Christians (disciples of Jesus), return to the Father, Son and Holy Spirit; our love. A love that first began, in the heart of God - was shared with the Son and Holy Spirit. Then shared with us, the people of this Earth, and finally that love is returned to the Father, Son and Holy Spirit.

The first commandment is not. You must attend Church regularly, or you must pray a minimum of four times a day or you must give a certain percent of your income to charity or....

These are significant signs a person considers himself or herself, a son or daughter of God.

Rather than focus on Church attendance or the number of prayers prayed or the amount of money to be given. The first commandment is to. "*Love* the Lord your God..." Matt 22:37.

Our love is what God the Father wants most from us. Yes he wants our worship and our service and our prayers; but first and foremost - he wants our love.

It is the same with Jesus. After Jesus had risen from the dead, he met Peter again. When Jesus met Peter again, the conversation should have been about the way Peter denied Jesus three times and Jesus should have berated Peter for denying him.

Instead of berating Peter or asking, "why did you deny me" (as most would   consider reasonable), Jesus simply asked Peter three times, "Do you love me?"

Jesus wants his disciples to obey him but first and foremost he wants us to love him, just as he loves us.

Then there is the third member of the trinity. Can we love the Holy Spirit? In my book called *The Holy Spirit,* I make the point that the Holy Spirit is a divine personal being - in the same way Jesus and God the Father; are divine, personal, beings.

Because the Holy Spirit is a divine person, we can love him too, even though we do not see him and do not have a ready image of him, as we do for Jesus.

Can you see the connections? Love starts in the heart of God. Is shared with the Jesus and Holy Spirit. Collectively they share their love with the people of this Earth. Then we, God's children/disciples of Jesus; share that love with all people, and finally. Return the love given us in the first place, to the Father/Son and Holy Spirit.

The rest of this book, continues in the same vein. Values that start in the heart of God, continue along the arms of the cross to the Son and Holy Spirit; then if we will allow it, work their way round the arms of the triangle, finally returning to the Father.

Here is a thought.

If we allow the infusion of God's love (and all the other values) to complete the circuit of the triangle, that infusion becomes a transfusion, and that transfusion becomes transformational!

Chapter 2

Oneness/unity

Jesus prayed this prayer for his disciples

"that they (the disciples) may be one as we are one." (We meaning, God and Jesus). John 17:11 NIV

 A number of times during his ministry Jesus conveyed the idea that he was "one" with the Father.

"If you knew me, you would know my Father also." John 8:19 NIV

"...the Father knows me and I know

the Father." John 10:15 NIV

"...when you see me, you are seeing the one who sent me." John 12:45 NLT

"Don't you believe that I am in the Father and the Father is in me." John 14:10 NIV

Saying after saying, all repeat the same message. Jesus, and God his Father, were one!

The Bible does not say explicitly that the Holy Spirit and God the Father are one also, but evidence from the Bible, points to that. The Apostle Paul wrote that *the* Holy Spirit is *from God."* 1 Cor 2: 12

 Any being created by God, has his nature and any being who is close to God, has his values. It is possible to see their common nature and values, from the following list that compares their natures and values.

God the Father::The Holy Spirit::The Son

Are Eternal

Gen 21:33   Heb 9:14   John 1:1

Creators

Gen 1:1   Gen 1:1   John 1:3

Have great power

Jude 25   Zech 4:6   Rev 19:16

Have feelings

Exod 3:7   Eph 4:30   John 11:35

Are Holy

Rev 4:8   John 14:26   John 4:34

Are Loving

Deut 7:7   Rom 15:30   John 11:5

Sources of peace

Phil 4:7   Gal 5:22   John 14:27

Counselors

Rom 11:34   John 14:16   Isa 9:6

Are Truth

Psa 31:5   John 14:17   John 14:6

That list is not exhaustive, but from the those verses, it is easy to see that the Holy Spirit and the Father, all share the same nature and values; because they are one.

The arms of the cross represent the unity of God the father, the Son and the Holy Spirit. IE. There is a unity or oneness.

That oneness or unity is also implied by Jesus command to take the Gospel to all the world and baptize new disciples in the "name of the Father, and the Son and Holy Spirit." Matt 28:19 GN

Baptism is not meant to be in the name of one member of the trinity, but all three. The three together, being one.

Side one of the triangle

When the Father/Son and Holy Spirit relate to us, they relate to us with a complete oneness of unity and purpose. Jesus said, "My food is to do will of him who sent me... John 4:34. When Jesus came to this Earth, he did not come to this Earth to do his own will. He came to do the will of his Father. He came to achieve the plans agreed with the Father, before he came.

Not only that, what Jesus taught us, were not his own insights, but those given him by God his father. He said

"For I gave them the words, you gave me...John 17:8 NIV.

Jesus was passionate about doing his Father's will and passing on what God had told him - but what about the Holy Spirit?

Before his trial, Jesus took the twelve disciples aside and gave them what could be called, a preparatory talk. It was a teaching session to prepare them, for when he was gone. During that preparatory, pre-crucifixion teaching session, Jesus indicated to the disciples about the way both He and the Holy Spirit were working in harmony to create the new Church.

"But I tell you it is for your good that I am going away. Unless I go away, the Counselor (Holy Spirit) will not come.... "John 16:7 NIV

The existence of the Church today, is the result of planned cooperation between Jesus and the Holy Spirit. Jesus came to lay the foundation, and the Holy Spirit came afterwards, to build on the foundation, Jesus had laid. There is a 'oneness' or unity in their actions.

However, even while Jesus was laying the foundations of the Church during his ministry, there was a 'oneness' with the Spirit. Luke tells us that Jesus only began his ministry when he returned from the time of testing, "full" of the Holy Spirit (Luke 4:1) and during his ministry, Jesus was full of joy through the Holy Spirit. Luke 10:21.

Once Jesus had ascended to heaven, it appears he left the building of the Church to the first disciples, and   the Holy Spirit. But even after he had returned to heaven, Jesus was still assisting with the   building   the Church.

Jesus appeared to a fanatical Pharisee called Saul on the road to Damascus, and asked him to become an Apostle whose primary task was to call Gentiles (non-Jews), to become disciples of Jesus.

And in the first chapters of the book of Revelation we read about Jesus assessment of seven churches in Asia. So it is not as if Jesus retired to heaven with the attitude, my job is done, now I can relax and leave everything to the Holy Spirit and the disciples.

Both during the ministry of Jesus and after he returned to heaven, Jesus and the Holy Spirit work in tandem – and are still working as a unified team for the unified task of establishing, then building the Church.

Then, if we roll the clock forward to the end of the era of the Church, there is a picture in the book of Revelation of the Holy Spirit and Jesus, 'still' working in tandem or unity of purpose. John wrote

> *"The Spirit and the bride (Jesus) say, Come!" Rev 22:17*

So the Holy Spirit has been and is working in tandem and harmony with Jesus, but also works in harmony with God's plans and purposes.

The Holy Spirit was there, working in tandem with God the father, when the World was created. Gen 1:1 The Holy Spirit was there for the beginning of Jesus' ministry and the birthday of the Church (the feast of Pentecost), and will be there for during the final era of the Church.

> "In the last days, God says I will pour out my Spirit on all people....."
> Acts 2:17

Oneness or unity, is a characteristic of all three members of the trinity. They value unity and work together in complete unity.

Side two of the triangle

The Father, Son and Holy Spirit work together in complete unity of purpose, and value unity or oneness among God's people/Christians. The Psalmist wrote.

> "How wonderful it is, how pleasant, for God's people to live together in harmony.... That is where the Lord has promised his blessing..." Psa 133: 1&4 GN

When God sees a unity among his people. When he sees even a close proximity to the unity that exists in heaven, God cannot help but be delighted and so, he sends his blessing on that unity.

Jesus likewise values unity/oneness among his disciples. He prayed that the disciples would be, "one". John 17:11 At that time Jesus was praying for those who would become Christians, when he prayed, Jesus could have prayed any number of things.

He could have prayed that future Christians would have, nice buildings. Or he could have prayed that they would have superb teaching or prayed that they have, first class organization Instead, Jesus prayed that they would be "one", just as he and God his father, were one.

We can see that same value on unity and oneness in Jesus' teachings about marriage.

- Marriage.

> "For this reason a man will leave his father and mother and be united to his wife, and the two will become one flesh. So they are no longer two, but one. Therefore what God has joined together, let man not separate." Matt 19:5-7 N.I.V.

Twice Jesus used the word "one" in those verses. Of the early church it was written.

> "All the believers were one in heart and mind. No one claimed that any of his possessions was his own...Acts 4:32 N.I.V

The early believers were of one; heart, mind and purpose.

The Apostle Paul, detecting some division in the Church at Ephesus wrote. "Make every effort to keep the unity of the Spirit through the bond of peace." Eph 4:3 NIV,

Side three of the triangle:

The Father/Son and Holy Spirit love to see a unity in God's people in whatever they do – be it prayer or worship.

> "I also tell you this: If two of you agree here in earth concerning anything you ask, my Father in heaven will do it for you. For where two or three gather together as my follower, I am there among them."
> Matt 18:19&20 NLT

It is not as if God does not hear or value our prayers, when we pray alone, but there is a special place in his heart for prayers in which, two or more agree - for it tells God the Father that his people are of one mind. That they are in unity, just as he is in unity with his Son and the Holy Spirit.

Chapter 3

Right/Righteous

There are various words in the Bible that convey the same value. Right, righteous, righteousness. To be righteous means to be "just" or "upright" or "honest". In the Greek language, the word righteousness is *Dikaiosune* and there are a number of possible meanings, depending on the context of the word. When used of God, it means, that which is in conformity with his nature. God is by nature; just, upright and honest.

It is not surprising that we find this same value, in all three members of the trinity.

- God is righteous.

    His decrees are righteous (Rom 1:32)
    His judgment is righteous (Rom 2:5)
    His acts are righteous (Dan 9:16)

- Jesus is righteous Acts 3:14

- The Holy Spirit is righteous. Rom 14:17

Side one of the triangle_

Down the first side of the triangle comes righteousness, to us. We Christians are made righteous by our faith. It is a gift from God, as a result of believing the Gospel message that Jesus died in our place, for our sins. Rom 3:22-23 The theological term for that is, imputed righteousness.

If any are unsure what imputed righteousness means, I make this analogy. Imagine you have just received your latest bank statement. On that statement are the amounts of various withdrawals and deposits. On most bank statements, besides each withdrawal or deposit, there is some indication of who the money went to, or came from.

While looking at your latest bank statement you notice a deposit in the column where deposits are recorded. But instead of a figure of say $200, there is a word in the deposit column, saying *righteousness*'.

Beside that word, are two other words which indicate who deposited that righteousness into our account. Those two words are simply, *love God*

That is the nearest way I can describe imputed righteousness. We, because of our faith in the redeeming death of Jesus, have been credited with a deposit of righteousness. A righteousness we will never be good enough to earn, or deserve.

Side two of the triangle

Righteousness comes below faith, hope and love in the hierarchy of Christian values but it is still, so important. I can recall a conversation with a Christian a number of years ago. This Christian worked for a major firm. At his firm, one of the senior accountants was a Christian who had worked at the firm for decades. He was trusted, not only because he had been a long time employee, but also because it was known that he went to Church most Sundays and to a church with a well earned reputation, for doing good in the community.

After it was discovered that this Christian accountant had been diverting significant funds to his own businesses, other Christians at the same firm did not mention they were Christians for about two years, such was the feeling of betrayal among management at the firm, at the actions of this long-time, Christian employee. In other words. From the perspective of the people who were not Christians at this firm.

They trusted this employee because he had been there for a long time, but an additional reason for their trust, was. He was a Christian who went regularly to Church. Take away righteousness from the faith, and it is not worth a lot.

Jesus lambasted the Pharisees for their 'self righteousness', but that does not mean that righteousness is, of any less value.

There are a number of consequences when Christians or any person does not value righteousness. The first casualty is self. Jesus called it, losing your soul.

The second casualty of unrighteousness, is relationships with other people. When a person's unrighteousness comes to light, the trust relationship they had with so many people, is usually damaged. Sometimes irreparably.

I am thinking of a family where there is now a zero relationship between the children and their father because of his unrighteousness. As someone who has had the privilege of having children, that cost would be virtually unbearable, if my children did not want anything to do with me.

The third casualty of unrighteousness, is our relationship to the Father/Son and Holy Spirit, both now and in eternity. Because they are holy and righteous, the degree to which we act unrighteously; will be the degree in which our relationship will deteriorate.

A person who acts unrighteously, can still go to Church and enjoy the corporate blessings, but there will not be any real relationship with the Father/Son and Holy Spirit.

David undoubtedly went to the Temple to worship after committing adultery, murder and deceit – and would have enjoyed with others the great festivals, but I am sure there was a heaviness to his worship. He was there, God was there, but not there – that is, until his sins those unrighteous acts of murder, deceit and adultery, were confessed.

God does not condemn us. Satan does that, however righteousness is part of God's nature and God sees unrighteousness from every angle.

The damage it does to a person's character which Jesus called, destroying your soul. The unfairness to others when we or others act unrighteously and finally. Unrighteousness affects our relationship with the Father/Son and Holy Spirit because they cannot deny who they are. Beings who are, holy and righteous.

Jesus had the right approach. He urged his followers to value and desire righteousness. He said "Blessed are those hunger and thirst for righteousness." Matt 5:6 NIV.

(1) A person who is blessed, is someone who knows God's favor. (Relationship with God)

(2) Righteousness enables us to sleep at night with a clear conscience and because we are living a righteous life. (Relationship with ourselves)

(3) Then there is our (relationship with others). Solomon wrote.

"A good reputation is better than expensive perfume...." Eccles 7:1 GN

A friend of mine regularly travels out of town on company business and submits receipts for his food, travel and accommodation expenses when he returns. Any receipts my friend hands in to his boss, are immediately passed to the accountant for payment without question or perusal.

 His boss does not even look at them or query them like he does other employees from the same firm, who travel out of town. That is because this manager is convinced about this Christian employee's integrity.

He has in Solomon's words, *"A good reputation."*

The prophet Isaiah painted a positive picture of a country, in which righteousness was characteristic of the lives of it's citizens.

> *Justice will dwell in the desert*
>
> *and righteousness live in the fertile field.*
>
> *The fruit of righteousness will be peace;*
>
> *the effect of righteousness will be quietness*
>
> *and confidence forever.*
>
> *Isa 32:16&17*

Did you notice the second to last word Isaiah

used, "confidence"? When people lie to or steal from or manipulate those close to them, trust is broken. When trust is broken or is uncertain, people are no longer confident of their relationship with the person/s they no longer trust.

When people are trustworthy, those close to them have confidence in them. They know they can rely on their word. They know they can trust them and that breeds confidence.

Side three of the triangle_

We cannot give God righteousness because God is already, totally righteous. But when we live righteous lives, that means we have, clear access to God.

When we come to worship, we come as people who live, righteously. In plain language, that means. When we come to God in worship; we will not have spent our weekdays; ripping people off or lying or manipulating them or surfing the internet for pornography or .

If we did, our lives would not be righteous and our worship, unacceptable. The prophet Isaiah explained the situation in his own words.

Behold, God's hand in not short.

Or his ear deaf

But your sins have hid his face from you. Isa 1:18

By contrast, if we are living a righteous life, then we have access to the throne room of God. James wrote. "The earnest prayer of a righteous person has great power...James 5:16 NLT

Chapter 4

Joy

- God has joy. Neh 8:10.

- Jesus had joy. Luke 10:21

- The Spirit has joy. Gal 5:22

Joy is part of the nature of God, I don't know why joy is part of the nature of God but perhaps it is natural in a place where there is no darkness and only light if left. Joy is part of God's nature, a joy he has shared with the his Son, and the Holy Spirit.

Joy is not a word used regularly today, so it is necessary to explain what this word means.

Most are familiar with the word 'happy' or 'happiness'. Happiness is an emotion a person feels when something good has occurred in their lives.

People become happy after they have won money or a competition or been promoted. People are likely to be happy after they have won a race or been part of a winning team. A person is likely to be happy if they have received an award for an outstanding performance in fields such as, science or drama or music.

By contrast, joy has nothing to do with winning prizes or receiving awards or suddenly getting rich. Joy is an emotion that comes from the very heart and nature of God, and occurs, when his purposes are fulfilled.

For example, when Mary the mother of Jesus came to visit her cousin Elizabeth, the baby inside her womb, "jumped for joy". Luke 1:44 NLT When an angel of the Lord appeared to some shepherds at the time of Jesus' birth, the Angel said, "I bring you good news that will bring great joy.....Luke 2:10 NLT

After Jesus had sent the disciples out on a trail mission trip, they returned saying: "Lord, even the demons obey us when we use your name." Luke 10:17 Luke, writing about that occasion,

"Jesus was filled with the joy of the Holy Spirit....Luke 1:21 NLT

Can you see, whenever the purposes of God are fulfilled, there is joy? A joy that is part of God's nature.

Side one of the triangle

> "The Holy Spirit gives us joy; as a fruit." Gal 5:22

> "...the joy of the Lord, is our strength." Neh 8:10

Side two of the triangle

After the disciples had returned from villages teaching/healing and setting people free from demons; Luke records. "When the seventy two disciples returned, they joyfully reported to him. Luke 10:17 Happiness comes from what we get, but joy comes through ministering to others and aligning with the purposes of God. When aid workers see children become healthy or receive an education, there is joy.

Side three of the triangle

Throughout the book of Psalms, David repeatedly uses the word joy, to describe his relationship to God. He wrote "Sing for joy" , "shout for joy". "Come, let us sing to the Lord! Let us shout joyfully to the Rock of our salvation. Let us come to him with thanksgiving. Let us sing psalms of praise to him." Psa 95:1-2 NLT

When we praise and worship God with joy, we are returning to God, an emotion that is part of his nature and which, the Holy Spirit has given us.

Chapter 5

Holiness

- God is holy. Rev 4:8

- Jesus is holy. Acts 3:14

- The Spirit is holy. John 14:26

The word holy is not defined in Bible commentaries. Most explanations simply say that something which is holy, is something which is dedicated to God. The holiness of God may be a reflection of the fact that he is total truth, is totally just, is totally righteous. A reflection of the fact that the love of God, is totally impartial. Combine total truth, total righteousness, total justice and total impartiality together in one being, and that being is uniquely, holy.

Side one of the triangle

God imputes or credits, holiness to us, through our faith in the atoning death of Jesus. Paul wrote,

> "Yet now he has reconciled you to himself through the death of Christ in his physical body. As a result, he had brought you into his own presence, and you are holy and blameless as you stand before him." Col 1:22 NLT

Side two of the triangle

> "For God saved us and called us to a holy life." 2 Tim 1:9 NLT

A holy life and a righteous life are one and the same. Paul wrote to the Christians at Thessalonica.

> "You are witnesses and so is God, of how holy and righteous and blameless we were among you... 1 Thess 2:10

Some examples of ways to live a holy and righteous life, were identified in the chapter about righteousness.

Side three of the triangle

> "In every place of worship, I want men to pray with holy hands lifted up to God, free from anger and controversy." 1 Tim 2:8 NLT

> "Worshiping God with holy hands and holy hearts and holy lives; is what is acceptable to God." C.f. Rom 12:1&2

Can you see the connections between the arms of the cross and the arms of the triangle. The Father/Son and Holy Spirit are, each holy. They impute holiness to us as a result of our faith.

We endeavor to live holy lives among the people we work and live with, and then finally. We worship and pray with holy hands and holy hearts to a holy God.

Chapter 6

Truth

- God of truth Psa 31:5

- Jesus is, the truth John 14:6

- ...the Spirit of truth John 16:13

Side one of the triangle

God's prophets continually spoke the truth to the people of their time. Often they did not like it, but it was the truth. Micah spoke these words (of truth) to some people of his time.

> "When you want a piece of land,
> you find a way to steal it.

> When you want someone's house
> you take it fraud and violence...
> "Micah 2:2 NLT

> "You have evicted women from
> their pleasant homes

> And forever stripped their children
> of all that God would give them."
> Micah 2:9 NLT

The prophet not only spoke truthfully about what God had seen, he also spoke a message of warning from God. :

> "But this is what the Lord says:
> I will reward your evil with evil...
> You will no longer walk around
> proudly ..." Micah 2:3

The prophet Nathan confronted David with the truth about his adultery, murder and deceit. Cleverly Nathan told a story to get King David to see the

David, to his credit, accepted the truth of what the prophet Nathan said and was finally honest with himself and with God, about his sins. He wrote

> "Surely you desire truth in the inner
> parts ..." Psa 51:6 NIV

God is a God of truth, speaks the truth

through his prophets and spoke through his Son, who is "the truth." John 14:6. But he also looks for that quality in our inner parts – meaning our mind and conscience .

During his ministry, Jesus often preceded what he was about to say, with these words, "I tell you the truth....." Jesus was continually telling the truth because it was part of his nature - a nature he had received from God his Father.

Jesus did not continually tell the truth because he wanted people to feel uncomfortable or condemned. Rather he told the truth because he wanted people to be free. John 8:32

And this is what we need to understand about truth. It is freeing. Freeing for us and freeing for others.

In the Bible, the prophets told the truth because they knew God wanted to end the yoke of injustice and murder and fraud, that bound the people and the country.

Along with the Father and Son, the Holy Spirit is also called, the "Spirit of truth." That is what Jesus called the Holy Spirit and something which should not surprise readers by now. All three sharing, exactly the same quality.

When Ananias and Saphira lied to the Apostles, Peter said "you have lied to the Holy Spirit." Acts 5:3 NIV IE. They had lied to the Spirit of truth.

Jesus, speaking of the Holy Spirit said, "he will guide you into all truth." John 16:13 NIV That is one of the key purposes of the Holy Spirit, to guide each Christian into truth. That is why we need the Holy Spirit.

Side two of the triangle

About the words we speak to one another, Paul wrote.

- Instead, we will speak the truth in love...Eph 4:15 NLT

- So let us celebrate the festival, not with the old bread of wickedness and evil but with the new bread of sincerity and truth. 1 Cor 5:8 NLT

Side three of the triangle

> "...those who worship him must worship him in spirit and in truth." John 4:24 NLT

The truth that began in the heart and nature of God, is returned to him when we worship "in Spirit and in truth."

Chapter 7

Faithfulness

- God is faithful. Deut 7:9 Psa 145:13

- Jesus was faithful and is called, faithful. Heb 2:17 Rev 19:11

- A fruit of the Spirit is faithfulness Gal 5:22

Side one of the triangle

Faithfulness is a characteristic of the Father/Son and Holy Spirit. They are faithful to us; even when we are unfaithful to them. 2 Tim 2:13

Jesus was faithful to Peter, even after Peter

had denied him three times. He was faithful to Peter by forgiving him and commissioning him to be the leader of the new Church. John 21:15-19

David wrote, "the faithfulness of the Lord endures for ever... Psa 117:2 NIV

God is faithful towards the faithful. "To the faithful, you show yourself faithful." Psa 18:25 NIV

Side two of the triangle

We are urged to be faithful in our dealings with our family, employers, church.

Paul urged slaves to work hard, not just when they are watching – which means to work faithfully, even when our employer is not watching. Col 3:23

Faithful to our marriage partners. 1 Tim 3:12 & 1 Tim 5:9

Faithful in ministry. Col 1:7

Side three of the triangle

We are to be faithful to Jesus and to God, the Father. In his letter to the Church at Ephesus, Paul called the Christians.. the faithful in Christ Jesus." Eph 1:1 NIV

Jesus told the parable of the sower to

encourage disciples to remain faithful. Jesus recognized that some who became his followers, would not remain faithful and fall away because of a number of reasons. When difficulties arise or when some are attracted by wealth. Matt 13:18-23

At the end of our life; Jesus would love to be able to say to us. "Well done, good and faithful servant!" Matt 25:23

Two things Jesus would like to say to us when we arrive at the gates of heaven. "Son/daughter, I know you have used your skills and opportunities, throughout your life. When you had success, you were tempted to let your faith slip away and concentrate on the success – but you remained faithful.

Or during times of great difficulty, you were tempted to throw in the towel of your faith when you could not understand why I allowed some things to occur - yet you have remained faithful to the end!

 Well done! Welcome to my Father's, fabulous house. Come and enjoy it forever!"

Chapter 8

Giving

- God is a giving God. He gave us his Son, life, a spirit, hope, peace, eternal life. 1 John 5:12

- Jesus was by nature giving and is by nature, giving: He gave us peace, God's words (John 15:15), eternal life (1 John 5:12) and gave himself as a ransom for us. Matt 28:20.

- The Holy Spirit is the giver of fruit and the gifts. Gal 5:22 & 1 Cor 12&14

The three members of the trinity are, by nature, givers!

Side one of triangle

> Jesus speaking … "my peace I give you". John 14:27

> He (God) gives strength to the weary... Isa 40:29

Jesus, speaking about himself said.

> "For even the Son of man came not to be served, but to serve others, and to give his life as a ransom of many." Matt 20:28 NLT

Serving and giving are basically the same thing. The Holy Spirit gives nine different fruits. The first three, *love, joy, peace* are for us to enjoy and which will hopefully rub off on those around us.

The second three fruits are the fruits *patience, kindness, goodness.* These are fruits to exercise in our relationships with other people. The last three *faithfulness, gentleness, self control* - help us both with our relationship with the Father and Son, and other people. Gal 5:22

The Holy Spirit also gives nine different gifts. I Cor 12: 7-10

Side two of triangle

> But when you *give* to the needy..
> Matt 6:3

> Freely, freely you have received,
> freely, freely *give*. Matt 10:8

> It is more blessed to *give* than
> receive. Acts 20:35

Italics added, in all three verses.

Being a giving person, is a natural part of being a Christian. How we give and what we give and when we give, will vary from Christian to Christian, and circumstance to circumstance.

Sometimes money, other times practical assistance. It could be as simple as offering a ride home when someone else's car is being repaired or a word of encouragement. Practical advice about...

There is no limit to the number of ways a giving person can give, if someone has, a giving attitude.

Side three of the triangle

Giving to God, stems from the Christian world view. A view that everything we have., was given to us by God in the first place. When

David and the Israeli people gave offerings and tithes to God, in David's view, when they gave,   they were simply giving to God what he had given them, in the first place. 1 Chron 29:13

In the book of Exodus we read

All the Israelite men and women who were willing brought to the Lord, freewill offerings for all the work the Lord through Moses had commanded them to do. Exod 35:29 NIV

The Apostle Paul had the same attitude. He wrote,

...."God loves a cheerful giver." 2 Cor 9:7 NIV

Praise and worship, are also acts of giving.

Let us rejoice and be glad and give him glory! Rev 19:7 NIV

Apart from giving of our money and our worship, the ultimate gift we can give to God, is ourselves. That is what the Apostle Paul encouraged the Christians at Rome to do. To offer or give themselves as a living sacrifice to God, holy and acceptable, which he called, "your spiritual worship." Rom 12:1&2

Chapter 9

Delight

- God delighted in his Son Jesus (Matt 12:18) and God the Father, delights in us. Isa 62:4 & Zeph 3:17

- Jesus delights in our life achievements . Matt 25:23

- The Spirit. The Bible does not specifically say that the Holy Spirit delights in us but it does tell us that we can "grieve", the Holy Spirit. Eph 4:30. In his letter to the Church at Ephesus, Paul listed words and actions that "grieve" the Spirit. Actions such as: stealing, telling lies, foul language and slander.

As well as listing actions that grieve the Spirit, Paul wrote about words and actions that, delight* the Holy Spirit. At least that is implied. It is implied that actions like: telling the truth, getting rid of anger, words of encouragement, being tender-hearted and forgiving one another, 'delight' the Holy Spirit.

Side one of the triangle

The word "delight" is embedded in my mind because it's use took me completely by surprise, about 15 years ago. At that time we were part way through a Church camp when a woman who was a counselor in our Church, came up to me and asked a question that took me, completely by surprise!

Completely by surprise because I had just completed a Discipleship manual that had about 1500 verses in it. Prior to writing the manual, I had reviewed the whole Bible and looked at approximately 3000 verses before settling on the 1500 verses that were included in the Discipleship Manal, collated into 113 different topics.

So it would be fair to say, "I knew the Bible as well as any Christian" and that no-one should have been able to surprise me by saying. "Are you aware of this subject or theme, in the Bible?"

Despite having the confidence that I knew the Bible as well as anyone and could comment on any subject or theme,   I was floored by the question this counselor asked me.   Her question was,

"Philip, do you know that God delights in you"

and she stood there, waiting for a response?

I was stunned by the question and did not know how to reply. Obviously when I had canvassed the whole Bible, I had not read those verses in Isaiah and Zephaniah in which the prophets told the people of Israel, God delights in you.

And in saying that, the prophets were very aware the people they were addressing these words to, was not a nation of saints! In fact, far from it. At times, reading the Old Testament can be a depressing because it seems to be a litany of the nations faithlessness, oppression and injustice to one another.

The prophets give us the impression that there were, 'very few' saints in the country. Despite that impression, both prophets said God "delights" in you" to both individuals and the nation.

Back to the camp, I could not reply to this

counselor with a yes or a no answer. Partly because I was stunned by the use of the word "delights" and partly because I had to think through my theology, so I said. "I will have to think about that!"

As I walked away, stunned by the question, I began to think about my theology up to that time. My theology was.

I know God loves me and he loves all people – for that is what the Bible tells me and I know that is true because his Spirit assures me, it is so. But the counselor did not use the word love, she used the word "delight".

I toyed with the thought, "delights in me?" In my thinking, that is a word that should be reserved for famous saints and   missionaries and notable Christian leaders. The likes of Mother Teresa and Dr Billy Graham but not for ordinary Christians, like myself.

At that time I was self employed in a one-man business, and apart from having written the Discipleship manual, I was just a normal member of a congregation of about 200, in the small country of New Zealand – near the ends of the Earth.

So there was nothing that distinguished me from any of the other 200 Christians in my congregation, or any of the world's 1.8 billion Christians. Or in a few words, there was nothing extraordinary about my Christian life that would cause God to say, 'I 'delight' in you! Instead of, I love you.

After the counselor posed that question, I spent the next 3-4 hours trying to think of reasons why God would merely love me, but delight in the famous Christians I mentioned.

In the end, I knew it was a lie, that God would make an exception for ordinary Christians, and distinguish between them, and the greats of the faith. In the end, I had to accept that, God "delights" in me also, which leads to the question.

"Do you know that God both loves you and delights in you?" I hope you believe it or if not, start praying "Lord, help me to both believe that you delight in me, just as you did the people of Israel; despite their faults.

Side two of the triangle

Early on in our marriage, my wife and I took Solomon's words to heart the words, "Delight in the wife of your youth...." Prov 6:18 KJ Although Solomon referred only to his wife, we took it to apply to both of us.

In those verses, Solomon was effectively

saying to readers. Have a one-track mind.

Keep it fixed on your wife or husband. Don't start gazing around at other men or women, as if the grass would be greener, if we were in a relationship with them. Someone, other than our marriage partner. More than that. Delight in him or her.

And taking our cue from Isaiah and Zephaniah, we should delight in our fellow Christians. The Apostle Paul began a number of his letters with these words. "To the saints..... E.g. Eph 1:1.

Now the use of the word 'saint', like the words "delights in you", is surprising because the Christians in the Church in Ephesus,   were hardly saints. 'Saints in the making' - maybe, but hardly saints, given what Paul later wrote in the same letter.

 After building them up and encouraging them in their faith during the first four chapters of his letter, in chapter five the Apostle begins to address some of the things they are doing and saying, that required changing.

He urged them to stop stealing, lying, slandering and using foul language. He urged them get rid of bitterness and rage and malice. Eph 5:28-30

Those words and actions, are not those of saints. Saints in the making, maybe. Saints on the journey with some way to go, yes. Yet that is what the Apostle called them, "saints."

He called them saints because they were redeemed by the precious blood of Jesus, and because they had claimed that redemption; so in God's eyes, they were saints.

By calling the Christians at Ephesus "saints', Paul was effectively saying, "I delight in you."

Side three of the triangle

David wrote, "Delight yourself in the Lord... " (Psa 37:4 NIV) and the prophet Isaiah wrote.

"I delight greatly in the Lord; my soul rejoices in God my savior. " Isa 61:10 NIV

Isaiah did not go the Temple regularly because, he had to. He did not pray regularly, because, he had to. He did not attend the great Jewish festivals because, he had to. He did not prophecy because, he had to. He did all these things because he *delighted greatly*, in his God.

Delight is something that begins in the heart and nature of God. It is found in Jesus his Son, and the Holy Spirit. They delight in us, as we, to the best of our ability try to be faithful disciples of Jesus. We in turn can delight in, our partners and fellow saints. Finally, the triangle becomes complete when we delight in, the Father/Son and Holy Spirit.

A delight in their God, is what motivated the great men and women, in the Old Testament,

Chapter 10

Humility

- God is humble. Exclaimed David. When I look at the night sky and see the work of your fingers ....what are mere mortals that you should think about them, human beings that you should care for them? Psa 8:4 NLT

- Jesus is humble. Paul wrote....he (Jesus) gave up his divine privileges*, he took the humble position of a slave and was born as a human being. Phil 2:7 NLT.

- The Holy Spirit is humble. The Holy Spirit was involved in creating the universe yet he will not force himself on us, even though he has the power, to do so. Instead of forcing himself on us, in humility he waits patiently for us to listen. And if we do not listen, he just grieves. C.f. Eph 4:30

Side one of triangle

The Father/Son and Holy Spirit are all, both amazing, and humble. They are the creators of the universe (John 1:1-2. Gen 1:2), and yet they think about and care for, mere mortal human beings like, you and I. C.f. Psalm 8

Side two of triangle

Paul wrote "Be completely humble and gentle.... Eph 4:2 NIV. In the book called *Humility,* a number of characteristics of humble people, are listed. Included in that list, are these indicators. The humble person is someone who will admit that they: are sometimes wrong and have made mistakes.

 That they don't always get, guidance right. A humble person will admit that they sometimes need the advice or the assistance of others. A humble person will graciously accept, gifts from other people. A humble person is someone who is happy to acknowledge the gifts and training and experience, of others.

The English word *humility* is a translation of the Greek word *Tapeinophrosyne*. Among the meanings of that word; are.

> *inasmuch as we are so, the correct estimate of ourselves.*

Another way of explaining what the word humility means is, 'to be on an even keel'. If we are on an even keel or have a correct estimate of ourselves, we will be open about our achievements, skills, training and gifts. But if we are on an even keel, we will not a let our boat lurch to one side and begin to get an inflated opinion of ourselves and begin to think that because we have certain skills and training, we are more important than any other crew members on the ship called *The Kingdom of God. Or* think we are more important than the goal.

God's goal for each of us, is do our part as crew members of the ship called, *The Kingdom of God.* Like any organization, we all have different roles and skills, but each is important – and the overall goal is to reach port (the end of the age).

On that day when the ship *The Kingdom of God* glides into it's final port, dazzling, as the bride of Christ; it will do so because each crew member has played his or her part, and used their gifts and; honored the other crew members for their contribution and team work.

Side three of triangle

> ".... and to walk humbly with your God." Micah 6:8 NIV

> "Humble yourselves before the Lord." Heb 4:10 NIV

> "The Spirit wants us to be humble and open, to be led by him." Rom 8:14

If the Earth's inhabitants realised how great and awesome God is, it would be unnecessary for Micah to write, "walk humbly with our God."

The most common title for Jesus in the New Testament is "Lord", and if he is not Lord of all, he is not Lord at all. We have the privilege of acknowledging Jesus as Lord now. One day acknowledging Jesus as Lord, will not be an option. One day in the future,

> " ... 'every' knee shall bow before him and confess that Jesus is Lord." Phil 2:11

At that time, every President and every Prime Minister. Every Olympic gold medalist, every CEO and every winner of the Oscars and Grammy Awards. Everyone, both great and small, 'will' acknowledge Jesus as Lord.

It seems to me, to be a smart move, to humble ourselves and acknowledge Jesus as Lord now - rather than wait for a time in the future when we, along with all other people, will have to acknowledge Jesus as Lord.

 Although I surrendered kingship of my life to Jesus, decades ago, I still find myself singing from time to time, the words of an old chorus.

"All to Jesus, I surrender. All to him I freely give. All to Jesus I surrender, I surrender all."

Those words speak to my psyche, my inner self and to Jesus, this message. "You are still, Lord! "

Chapter 11

Trust

- God is trustworthy. Prov 3:5&6

- Jesus is trustworthy. John 6:68

- The Holy Spirit is trustworthy. Luke 1:13*

*This verse implies that the Holy Spirit who is, God's ultimate gift, is trustworthy.

Side one of the triangle

God trusts us with his creation. He has given us dominion (trusted us) with authority over the Earth the animals and plants .Gen 1:26

Jesus entrusted to the first disciples and all of us who have followed, the spreading of the Gospel and making disciples. That trust is implicit in the words of what we call, the *Great Commission* Matt 28: 18-20.

Jesus also entrusted the first disciples, and by implication all of us who have followed, with the building of the Church. It is the same with spiritual gifts. The Holy Spirit entrusts his gifts to each one of us for the common good. 1 Cor 12:7-11

Side two of the triangle

Jesus told the parable of the talents to encourage disciples to use their talents. He praised ("Well done good and faithful servant.") those who used their talents and was severe on those who buried them. Matt 25:14-30

In that parable, Jesus referred to a talent, which was a coin used at those times. However, for those of us who speak English, it is an appropriate word because Jesus was urging us to use our talents (meaning skills and gifts and training), using money, as an illustration.

Trust-worthy leaders. 1 Tim 3:1-13 The Apostle Paul set a very high standard for leaders. Included among the characteristics he listed were that they should be: temperate, self controlled, hospitable, have a clear conscience and not be conceited or quarrelsome. Paul was basically saying, I would like Christian leaders to be 'trustworthy'.

Being trustworthy is so important. It is part of the nature of the Father/Son and Holy Spirit. A nature they share with us. And we too, will ideally be people who are trust worthy. I have had the privilege of spending most of my working life, working in secular occupations.

I have noticed how, subconsciously, people in the different places of employment, have divided their fellow employees into two groups.

Those they can trust and those they don't feel they can trust.

I wrote in an earlier chapter about a Christian accountant who embezzled a company's money, which resulted in, jail for the Christian accountant, but for other Christians it meant a difficult period of time.

 For the word "Christian" was associated with people who believe in God and try to do good to their fellow employees and fellow citizens, but are a people who; despite their outward appearances and religious profession, cannot be trusted.

Being trusted and trustworthy (like Jesus and God our Father) is vital for any successful relationship.

Side three of the triangle

> "Trust in the Lord, with all our heart
> for guidance." Prov 3:5

> "Do not let your hearts be troubled.
> Trust in God, trust also in me."
> John 14:1 NIV ~ said by Jesus

God asks us to trust him. Jesus asks us to trust him in both the good times and bad. The prophet Habakkuk listed a variety of circumstances that could occur. We might say today that if all these occurred, life had turned to custard,. Yet Habakkuk resolved to trust God despite all these possible calamities. Hab 3:17-19

They (the Father/Son and Holy Spirit) look for people who exercise their faith or trust; and they honor such people. Jesus honored a Roman centurion for his faith, suggesting that the Roman Centurion, had more faith than anyone else in Israel. Matt 8:10

Chapter 12

Generosity

- God is a generous God. Eph 2:4 James 1:5

- Jesus is generous. He spoke about giving generously. Luke 6:38

- The Holy Spirit freely bestows on us, the gifts and love of God.

Side one of the triangle

The trinity are generous with us.

...the incredible wealth of his grace and kindness toward us...Eph 2:7 NLT

And may you have the power to understand, as all God's people should, how wide, how long, how high, and how deep his love is. Eph 3:18 NLT

He generously poured out the Spirit upon us through Jesus Christ our Savior. Titus 3:6 NLT

If you need wisdom, ask our generous God. James 1:5 NLT

Side two of the triangle

We are to be generous with others.

... the godly are generous givers. Psa 37:21

Give freely and become more wealthy. Prov 11:24 NLT

The generous will prosper; those who refresh others will themselves be refreshed. Prov 11:25 NLT

Side three of the triangle

God loves a cheerful giver. 2 Cor 9:7

God loves it when we are generous in our giving, and with our love and praise.

Chapter 13

Relationship

- God wants a covenant relationship, with everyone who will respond. 1 Chron 28:9

- Jesus wants a relationship with us. Rev 3:2

- We can have fellowship with the Holy Spirit. 2 Cor 13:14

People do not understand the Bible (and Christianity), if they think that the Christian faith is merely a series of propositional truths, which people either believe, or don't believe. Or being a Christian means, attending a service of worship on Sunday and then, after the service is finished,   our 'religious obligations for the week, are completed.

Those are important aspects of the Christian life, but far from the complete picture. Before the fall, Adam and Eve had a natural and unhindered relationship with God, 24/7 – 365 days a year. As a result of their disobedience, that natural and unhindered relationship was broken, but not irreparably. Ever since then, the desire of the Father/Son and Holy Spirit has been that we humans live in a restored relationship with them.

Side one of the triangle

God's relationship with human beings is formalized in what is called, a covenant relationship. We speak of the Bible as comprising of the Old and New Testaments, when really we should be calling each part, the Old and New Covenants, because that is what the word Testament, means. See also Gal 4:24

In the Bible there were various covenants. There was also a covenant between God and his people. The essence of that covenant is found in Jeremiah's words.

"Obey me and I will be your God and you will

be my people." Jer 7:23 NLT God promised that all would go well his people, if they stayed in a covenant relationship with him.

The nearest modern day equivalents to a covenant,   is the commitment of two people in a marriage ceremony, to share, all of their lives together.

Through prophets like Isaiah, God spoke of his desire to have a relationship with his people both individuals and the nation.

"Come to me with your ears wide open. Listen and you will find life. I will make an everlasting covenant with you. I will give you all the unfailing love I promised to David." Isa 56:3 NLT

Through those words, God was saying:

- Come to me

- you will find life

- I will make an everlasting covenant with you

- I will give you unfailing love

Jesus was on the same plane said,

> "Come to me, all you who are
> weary and burdened...." Matt 11:30

Note, Jesus did not say come to Church if you are weary and burdened. Or read the Bible if you are weary or burdened. Rather he said, "Come to me... Both then and now, Jesus wants a relationship with his disciples. See Rev 3:20.

Jesus conveyed the same idea when he called the first disciples from their nets and tax collectors booth. When he called them, he did not say. "Read these teachings, consider them for a while and then, if you are happy with them, you may like to consider becoming one of my disciples." He did not say, "come and listen to me preach at the synagogue." Rather, he said,

"Come, follow me...

That is what Jesus wanted then, and wants now – a relationship with his disciples.

People do not understand the Holy Spirit if they think he is merely a power. The Holy Spirit does bring power, but first and foremost, he is a person. A divine person, like Jesus and God the Father.

Evidence for the Holy Spirit being a divine-personal-being is found in the book called *The Holy Spirit.* Because the Holy Spirit is a person, we can have fellowship with him and he with us. Paul wrote,

> "May the grace of the Lord Jesus Christ, the love of God and the fellowship of the Holy Spirit be with you all." 2 Cor 13:14.

The Holy Spirit wants to be close to us but if we turn away from him, that grieves him. Eph 4:30 He wants to be a friend and helper, in so many ways. To lead us, to assure us of God's love, to teach us....   Rom 8:16 & Rom 8:14 John 14:26

Side two of the triangle

Over 70 times the two words 'one another' are found in the New Testament. That means, we do not go to Church, just to worship God. We do not go to Church, just to make up the numbers in the service.

Being a Christian means to be in a series of relationships. A relationship with the Father/Son and Holy Spirit and, with our fellow travelers (Christians).

The many 'one anothers' found in the New Testament emphasis that Christianity is a journey to be shared, with others. Following on is a sample of some of the 'one anothers', found in the New Testament. All the verses quoted,   are from the NIV version of the

Bible.

- Be devoted to one another   ...Rom 12:10

- Honor one another...Rom 12:10

- Live in harmony with one another...Rom 12:16

- Accept one another....Rom 15:7

- ....stop passing judgment on one another. Rom 14:13

- Greet one another.. 1Cor 16:20

- ...serve one another. Gal 5:13

- ...be patient, bearing one another... Eph 4:2

- Be kind and compassionate to one another...Eph 4:32

- Encourage one another ...Heb 3:13

- ...love one another deeply... 1 Pet 1:22

The authors of those verses intended each of these 'one anothers' to be applied to people in our congregation, but they need not stop at the walls of our Church. Some of our friends for example, may worship in other Churches.

Jesus does not think denominationally as many Christians do, and is not concerned about the different names of Churches, or their varying emphasis. He wants us to love and encourage and serve, 'any' Christian, regardless of which church they belong to. That is kingdom thinking rather than, denominational thinking.

There is another sphere that these 'one anothers' can be applied to. In fact, I suggest that these 'one anothers' ought to be applied in this sphere first, then down at our local Church and in the wider church, secondly. That sphere is called 'our home', or wherever we live.

If these 'one anothers' were applied on a consistent basis to a marriage relationship or any close relationship, there would be little need, for counselors.

Side three of the triangle

We Christians have the privilege of a relationship with all three members of the trinity, 24/7, through our quiet times and during our services of worship. When the Apostle Paul wrote "pray at all times", he was meaning, we have the privilege of a relationship with God and with Jesus; any-time, anywhere.

It could be in the car or in a kitchen or office or factory or farm or sport's field or.... just anywhere.

For the Muslim, prayer is five times a day and requires facing Mecca. For the Christians it is different and is a result of different faith-view. That faiith view is;

"in him we live and move and have our being." Acts 17:28 NIV

Anyone who embraces that faith-view, will realise that Christians do not have to be at a Temple or in a Church or at an altar, to have a relationship with God - for God is, every where we live and move, and he is open, 24/7.

A true relationship is,   two-way. That means in our two-way relationship with God, we tell him our concerns. Then, because it is a two-way relationship, we wait for that still quiet voice so that the Father or Son can to tell us what is on, their heart.

That is what a true relationship is. Head to head and heart to heart.

Chapter 14

Just

The word just and justice are closely related. A just person practices justice. A just person is impartial.

- God is just. Dan 4:37 & Psa 99:4

- Jesus is just. Isa 9:7

- The Holy Spirit is just*

The Bible does say specifically   that the Holy Spirit is just, but the Bible tells us that the Spirit is "from God" or "of God". So it is inevitable that the Holy Spirit is just, because any being close to God and created by God, will share his values.

The passage 1 Corinthians 12:1-11 implies that the Holy Spirit gives the gifts justly and impartially.

Side one of the triangle

God and Jesus and the Holy Spirit, treat each person equally, impartially and justly. The author of the book of Deuteronomy wrote that God "shows no partiality and cannot be bribed." Deut 10:17

When Jesus was on Earth, the religious leaders were amazed at the way Jesus had time for everyone and treated everyone equally, and was not swayed by anyone; including themselves.

Side two of the triangle

The prophet Micah wrote. "And what does the Lord require of you? To act justly and to love mercy...." Micah 6:8 NIV

Unfortunately, in some developing countries there is a lot of corruption and injustice. Christian aid agencies wisely avoid getting involved in combating the corrupt and unjust systems and officials. They choose to help those disadvantaged by corrupt and unjust systems and officials, by providing advice, and loans   and assistance with microbusinesses so that individuals and families can have a future as a result of their own efforts, and in spite of, the unjust systems and officials.

Sometimes doing justice, may mean, seeking justice for others. A friend went to a tribunal hearing to speak for people whose second language was English and who were not fully familiar with the laws of the land. He did this because he could see that this family of fairly recent immigrants, were going to come off second best against a citizen whose first language was English and who was in my friend's opinion, using his familiarity with the English language and the laws of the land, to make unreasonable demands.

Side three of the triangle

God is just. That is a welcome part of his nature. He treats every person on this Earth, justly or fairly. Deut 10:17 God who is just, has no favorites which means. Anyone can come to him, regardless of any criteria like nationality, gender, race or occupation or whether we are a success or failure in the eyes of others.

God, being just, does not take any of those factors into consideration and just says, 'start talking. I love you."

When we come to God, we do not need to wait till we are perfect, before we come. We do not need to wait till we begin to attend church regularly (though that is usually helpful), before we come to God. He wants us to come, just as we are!

Jesus did not call, already perfect people, to become his followers. One was a cheating tax collector. Another a zealot who would happily murder a lone Roman; and another, prone to doubt (Thomas). All of the twelve would run like scared rabbits before his arrest, at a time when, he needed their support, most!

One of Jesus' female disciples was called Joanna. Luke 8:3 She was the wife of the manager of King Herod's household. To be the manager of Herod's house meant being a person, not too concerned about right or wrong - the disappearance of this person or that person or the manipulation of this person or that person.

 And Joanna, as wife of the manager, not too concerned that her husband was working for probably, the most unscrupulous employer in the land. Yet she became one of Jesus' disciples.

These examples mean, we come to God, just as we are! We become disciples of Jesus, just as we are, but once the journey has started and if we will allow it, Jesus will move us on from there, to become more like him. As we continue to have a relationship with the Father and Son, we will gradually become more like Jesus. That process is called sanctification.

The just nature of God will be welcome for all people when they stand in judgment before him. ..each of us will give a personal account to God. Rom 14:12 NLT See also Heb 12:23

Coming before God at the end of their life, will also be people who have not heard the words of the Bible, or the Gospel. So how will God judge, these people.

We do not know exactly, but we do know two things about God. He knows everything (Psa 139) and is just. So God will judge in a just way that takes into account that some knew nothing or very little, about the commands and values of the Bible.

Chapter 15

Wisdom

- God is wise Rom 11:33

- Jesus is wise Revelation 5:12

- Holy Spirit is wise 1 Cor 12:8

Side one of the triangle

"For the Lord grants wisdom." Prov 2:6 NLT

God gives wisdom to those who ask. 2 Chron 1:10 & James 1:5

Side two of the triangle

Jesus urged his followers to be, "wise as serpents and harmless as doves." Matt 10:16 KJ

We are to live wisely. Ephesians 5:15

Solomon wrote most of the proverbs in the book of Proverbs. In that book, are many wise sayings or proverbs. Solomon valued wisdom so much that he personified it. He wrote,

"Wisdom shouts in the streets. She cries out in the public square." Prov 1:20 NLT

Side three of the triangle

Our relationship to God is based on God's wisdom. Eph 2:8&9 See also Prov 3: 5&6

See also Psalm 51:6 and Psalm 111:10

Chapter 16

Peace

- God is a God of peace. Rom 15:13 8:10

- Jesus has peace. John 14:27

- A fruit of the Spirit is peace. Gal 5:22

Side one of the triangle

God gives us peace. "Grace and peace to you from God our father...1 Cor 1:3 NIV

Jesus speaking. "My peace I leave you; my peace I give you....John 14:27 NIV See also Col 3:15

One of the fruits the Spirit gives to us, is

peace. Gal 5:22

NB I sometimes get amazed at the number of Christians who turn to Eastern meditative practices, to find a sort of, semi peace. By emptying their minds, they find an absence of stress, but that is not anything like the peace of God.

 Why people to turn to the true source of peace, they find, real peace?

How do we find that peace. We turn our hearts toward God and toward Jesus, and begin to be still" Psa 37:7. And as we begin to be still and focus our thoughts on our creator or savior; we begin to experience, peace – true peace.

We begin to experience that peace, not because Jesus or God the Father have thought. 'Ah, Ryan or Sally have begun to pray and turn their thoughts towards me, so I will go to the room where we keep peace stored, and bring a little out, and give it to them as a reward for turning their thoughts towards me.'

Rather, we begin to experience peace, simply because we are tuning into beings who have incredible peace, as part of their nature. John 14:27 & Rom 15:10

Why travel down the street to buy the dried flowers at the shop called *Eastern meditative practices*,   when there are beautiful, fresh, scented flowers, in your Christian back yard?

Side two of the triangle

...live at peace with everyone. Rom 12:18 NIV

Blessed are the peacemakers. Matt 5:9 NIV

Side three of the triangle

We cannot give God peace because heaven, is full of it, but we can be 'at peace with God' because the wall of hostility has been broken down. Col 1:20

Saul of Tarsus went from being an angry Pharisee opposed to Jesus, to one who was for Jesus, and found peace with him.

Chapter 17

Patient/patience

- God is patient. Rom 2:4

- Jesus was patient. Luke 9:41

- A fruit of the Spirit is patience. Gal 5:22

Side one of the triangle

For many years you were patient with them...Neh 9:30 NIV

"Don't you see how wonderfully kind and tolerant and patient God is with you." Rom 2:4 NLT

Side two of the triangle

Love is patient, love is kind...1 Cor 13:4 NIV

... be patient, bearing one another in love. Eph 4:2 NIV

Side three of the triangle

"Be still in the presence of the Lord, and wait patiently for him to act." Psa 37:7 NLT

"You too must be patient. Take courage, for the coming of the Lord is near." James 5:8

Chapter 18

Bless

God is a blessing God. The word 'bless' and it's derivatives, 'blessing' 'blessed' 'blessedness' 'blessing', are found over 400 times in the Bible.

The Hebrew word *Berakah,* often translated into English as the word "bless", has a number of possible meanings. Included in those meanings are: *Blessing, benediction, benefit, gift, favor.* The word approximates the word *salom,* peace, welfare. P1508. NIV Study Bible

 At Jesus' baptism, God let those standing

there know that he well pleased with Jesus – and that Jesus had, his favor. At that time a voice from heaven said,

"This is my dearly loved Son, who brings me great joy." Matt 3:17 NLT

God was effectively blessing his Son.

The nature of the Holy Spirit is to give gifts. 1 Cor 12: 7 & 11 Someone who wants to bless others, may choose to give gifts, just like the Holy Spirit does.

Side one of the triangle

The Father, Son and Holy Spirit, bless us in so many ways. Through the gift of life, the gift of eternal life, through their love and through material blessings. The Holy Spirit blesses us and others through us, by giving us the gifts, and the fruits he has.

Side two of the triangle

God promised to bless all the people of the Earth through Abraham and Sarah. Gen 12.4

In the Bible, spoken words are considered to have the power to create. Though God sometimes speaks directly to people, often he chooses to bless people, through the actions and words, of other people. That is why God instructed Aaron to speak the following words of blessing to the people of Israel.

'May the Lord bless you
and protect you.
May the Lord smile on you
and be gracious to you.
May the Lord show you his favor
and give you peace.
Num 6:24-26 NLT

When the Church began, the believers shared their (blessings) of wealth and food with one another. Acts 2:44

Side three of the triangle

Amazing as it seems, we can bless God. The Hebrew word *Barak* is translated into English as either "Bless" or "Praise". C.f. Ps 13:1. Wrote David, "all my inmost being praise (or bless) his holy name.

Turn to the latter part of the book of Psalms and repeatedly the words "Praise the Lord..." are found. The word praise is synonymous with the word 'bless', so David was continually, blessing God.

When Jesus entered Jerusalem before his trial, spontaneously those beside the road began to shout and sing,

"Blessings on the King who comes in the name of the Lord." Luke 19:38 NLT

In services of worship, whether   with our words or our thoughts or our hands; we can bless the Lord. Equally when we do that when we are alone – and can, bless the Lord.

Chapter 19

Freedom

- God gives freedom Psa 116:16

- Jesus gives freedom John 8:36

- The Spirit gives freedom 2 Cor 3:17

Side one of the triangle

It was on God's heart to free his people from slavery to other nations, that is why he called people like Moses   and Gideon   and Nehemiah; to help free his people.

Salvation is free gift of God. Eph 2:8

Jesus said,

"if the Son sets you free, you will be free indeed." John 8:36 NIV

When we come into a relationship with Jesus, we experience that freedom. We also come to him, to ask him to break any bondage in our lives.

Freedom is associated with living his teachings. See John 8:31 When we begin to give, we are freer people. When we begin to forgive, we are freer people. When we begin to love God instead of things, we are freer people

Where the Spirit is, there is freedom. 2 Cor 3:17 Why not invite the Holy Spirit to fill you afresh? When he comes, there is freedom.

Side two of the triangle

Several hundred years ago God put it on the heart of English Christian and politician, William Wilberforce, to agitate for the abolishment of slavery - to set slaves free.

The goal of some Christians today, is to free children from child labor and the sex trade.

Some of the people we know, are bound up in chains. Jesus is the one who can provide freedom. Further becoming a disciple of his and beginning to live his teachings, will provide, further freedom. See the previous page about giving and forgiving and loving.

Side three of the triangle

In the Old Testament, offerings at the great festivals were called, "freewill" offerings. Those words, "freewill offerings" occur, 23 times in the Bible.

God loves it when we freely offer him some of our income, our time, our possessions and lives. That was the essence of what Paul wrote to the Church at Corinth.

"You must each decide in your heart how much to give. And don't give reluctantly or in response to pressure. For God loves a person who gives cheerfully." 2 Cor 9:7

Chapter 20

Light

This is the only chapter in which there are multiple meanings for the same word. IE. Light. In the Bible the word "light" is used literally, metaphorically and theologically.

"The commands of the Lord are radiant, giving light to the eyes." Psa 19:8 NIV

"God is light; in him there is no darkness at all." 1 John 1:5

The context of that verse from the book of First John, is the subject of sin and it's opposite, sinlessness. Darkness is equated with sin, and light with sinlessness – the state in which God exists.

Literally: God and every being in heaven, are bathed in, incredible light. There is no need for chandeliers in heaven or banks of high-powered lights, to illuminate it. Heaven is a place, filled with the light of the glory of God.

The Apostle Paul described the light surrounding God's throne, this way....."who lives in unapproachable light." 1 Tim 6:16 NIV The prophet Ezekiel described the light surrounding God's throne as a "brilliant light" and also a "radiance". Ezek 1:27&28

Metaphoric and theological: Two themes recur in the Bible, in regard to light.

<u>God is light.</u>

Wrote David, "The Lord is my light... Psa 27:1 NIV

<u>God's words are light</u>

"The unfolding of your words gives light...Psa 119:130 NIV

<u>Jesus is 'the' light</u>

John 1:3-9

<u>Jesus words (teachings) give light</u>

John 8: 12&31

The Holy Spirit is enveloped in light, because he lives in heaven, where God is. Appropriately, when he revealed himself at the feast of Pentecost, it was as tongues of fire. Fire produces, both warmth and light. The Holy Spirit is also pictured in the Bible as being like, "a refiners fire".

Side one of the triangle

When Jesus came incarnate into our World, his coming was described as bringing both life and light.   See John 1: 4-5. When Jesus began his ministry, he moved to the town of Capernaum, in the region of Zebulun and Naphtali. Matthew wrote,

.."the people who sat in darkness have seen a great light. And for those who lived in the land where death casts it's shadow, a light has shined." – meaning Jesus. Matt 4:16 NLT

The word light (in Matthew) is translated from the Greek word *Phos.* That word conveys the idea of something that gives off light, in the same way the moon reflects light.

Jesus was the light but also his words bring light (revelation), to darkened minds.

Side two of the triangle

In the introductory paragraphs, dual understandings were identified. God is light and his word is light. Jesus is the light, and his teachings bring light. Amazing though it is, that same dualism is used to describe us, his disciples. Jesus said

"You are the light" Matt 5:14

and

Our good deeds are light Matt 5:16

When some Jewish people rejected the Gospel message, Paul said to them, "the Lord has commanded us:

I have made you a light to the Gentiles that you may bring salvation to the ends of the earth." Acts 13:47 NIV

So it is both through who we are, and the message of salvation that we speak, that brings light to those around us.

Side three of the triangle

"But if we walk in the light as he is in the light, we have fellowship with one another, the blood of Jesus purifies us from all sin." 1 John 1:7 NIV

We can't give light to God but we can walk in

his light, provided we confess our sin. See . 1 John 1:9

I suggest that God is pleased when he looks down from heaven and sees his daughters and sons, reflecting light to the people of this Earth - much like the moon reflects light from the Sun. God is pleased to see that light reflected because he knows the light he sees being reflected, originated in his nature.

Chapter 21

Hope

God is a god of hope Jer 17:13

Jesus is our hope 1 Tim 1:1

Holy Spirit provides hope Rom 5:5

Side one of the triangle

...the God of hope fill you with joy and peace. Rom 15:13 NIV

Then you will overflow with confident hope through the power of the Holy Spirit. Rom 15:13 NLT

Side two of the triangle

If we are a Christian, we will provide hope for others. Anyone who blesses or encourages or assists or advises people who require advice or counsels, provides hope for someone else.

They are so many ways we can provide hope to people who seem to have a problem; wither through our support, through advice or through practical assistance.

Then Church leaders can provide hope for people in their daily lives, through. Preaching hope-filled, faith-filled sermons that both touch the lives of people in their congregations and link them to the God of, endless hope.

People working for Christian aid agencies provide hope that people can access medical care, or have clean water, or find meaningful employment or gain an education.

Side three of the triangle

...my hope is in you all day long. Psa 25:5

No one whose hope is in you will ever be put to shame. Psa 25:3

In the Hebrew and Greek, the word hope is much stronger in the than it is in English. In the Hebrew the word *Qawah* (which is usually translated 'hope' in English) means to "expect" or "wait for". It is a confident expectation not the, maybe he will - maybe he wont, type of attitude.

Concluding Thoughts

By now it will be obvious to readers that who God is, Jesus is; and what God is, the Holy Spirit is. All three share exactly the same nature and the same values. It will also be obvious that every value they have, they share with us. IE. Down the first side of the triangle (the highway from heaven) come to us; love and truth and holiness and peace and blessing; and all the other values mentioned in this book.

And, if I have made the case well we will share those same values we have received, with other people. And then, return to the

Father and Son and Holy Spirit what began in his heart and nature of God.

There are only three values which I can think of, that cannot complete the full circuit of the triangle. They are, grace and mercy and forgiveness. We cannot forgive God because God has not wronged us. We cannot show mercy to God. He does do not need our mercy and we cannot show grace to God because grace is shown by someone more powerful and deserving, to someone less powerful and, less deserving.

Even though grace and mercy and forgiveness cannot complete the circuit of the triangle, they can go around the circuit, as far as other people for they are an integral part of the Christian faith and life.

There is a possible addition to the symbols of the cross and triangle, one that could be added to the bottom line of the triangle. That additional line could be compared to a no-exit side-road.

 At the end of this no-exit side-road is our self. That side-road to our self has been included because, at least three values mentioned in this book can travel up the side-road to our self. One of these values is love.

To love ourselves, was part of the new commandment Jesus created. To "love your neighbor as you love yourself." Matt 22:39

We are beautiful in God's sight and valuable to Jesus. Even though that is true, no one can make anyone, love our self. We have to, choose to do that.

Loving one self does not mean to be in love with one self. It means valuing who we are as a unique individual, among over 7 billion people.

Another value that does the circuit of the triangle and which may need to travel up the side-road to our self is truth. Sometimes, for our own good, we need to be honest with ourselves. To speak the truth to ourselves.

David (after being confronted about his deceit, murder and adultery) finally began to be honest with himself. He wrote.

> "For I know my transgressions, and
> my sin is always before me...Surely
> you desire truth in the inner parts.
> Psa 51: 3&7 NIV

Hopefully it will be unnecessary to bring truth up that side-road to self, but I suspect, all of us from time to time need to be honest with ourselves about something. For me recently, it was pride. Pride in how much I could achieve in a given day and week. So proud in fact that I was overlooking the fact that I was over-loading my life to the point where I could not function properly. At the point of burn-out, I had to be honest or truthful, with myself.

It could be about an addiction we are not admitting. It could be about the way we are destroying those close to us, with our words or actions.

A woman in our Church who (in her 50's) shared recently how she was finally being honest with herself and with others, but it had taken most of her life, to get to that point. For her, finally being honest with herself and others, was liberating.

Two other values that we may need to allow up the side-road to our self, are grace and mercy. At the time of writing, my wife and I are laughing at ourselves (rather than berating ourselves) about the number of times we have either forgotten something, made a mistake or accidentally broken something – when tired.

Because of the stresses of life and because we are all fallible, sometimes we need to extend, grace and mercy to ourselves. You, I, everyone; makes mistakes and occasionally, large mistakes.

When we do, don't shoot yourself in the foot (colloquially speaking). Just admit that, like everyone else, we can make mistakes and if necessary, show grace and mercy to your self.

Jesus did not condemn Peter for denying him. He reminded Peter of his denial but did not condemn him for it. Sometimes we need to look at ourselves through Jesus' eyes and say. "I am not perfect and never will be, but Jesus still believes in me. I am going to learn from my mistakes, be gracious to my self and continue to be one of his disciples because; Jesus is gracious to everyone, including me."

To reiterate some of the key themes from this book.

1. The Christian faith is a whole. As the Apostle Paul wrote to the Church at Ephesus. ...."one Lord, one faith, one baptism and one God and Father of all who is over all and through all and in all. Eph 4:5-6

    The faith is one whole - a concept I have spent a whole book trying to convince readers. God's nature and Jesus's nature and the nature of the Holy Spirit; are one.

That same nature and the same values are infused into their relationship with us. Ideally into our relationship with one another and finally our relationship with the Father/Son and Holy Spirit.

2. Because the faith is one whole, that means what we believe and what we do, are one and the same! IE. What we believe about the nature of God, is meant to be a description of what we do (how we live),   day by day.

3. We were created for and designed to be, vessels of God's nature and values.

When we do so, I am sure it brings great pleasure to the heart of God.

If any person allows an infusion of the values that begin in the heart of God to complete the circuit of the triangle, that infusion becomes a transfusion, and that transfusion becomes, transformational!

One final thought. Every value identified in this book like *love* and *joy* and *peace* and *justice* and *freedom* and *truth* and *holiness*, are found in measureless quantities, in the place we call heaven. There they will not only be measureless, but they will be continuous!

Those thoughts are background to Paul's statement, "O death, where is your sting." When a person we know dies, and goes to heaven, naturally we who remain, grieve over their loss – but for the person who has gone to be with the Lord – to be in place of total and continuous; light and love and peace and righteousness and freedom and health....

Words are inadequate to describe such a place that exists beyond this life of stresses and rest. Victory and defeat. Loss and gain.

About Philip Watson

 I have grown up and live in New Zealand - Aotearoa (the Land of the Long White Cloud), currently residing in Auckland, our largest city with a population around 2 million people.

Around half of all New Zealanders live in Auckland. It is here that I can find the time to reflect on my faith and write.

It is the Bible and an intelligent and informed explanation of it's contents, that is the wind in the sails of the books I write. I am unashamedly evangelical or charismatic in my faith and my writings.

After finishing Theological College in New Zealand, I traveled to the Middle East to walk in the footsteps of Jesus, to glean a glimpse of the life he would have lived on this earth and soak in the ambiance of the world of Jesus and the glory of God's creations. This was for me a discovery of God and how important my Christian faith is for me, my family and my life.

I enjoy telling stories in my books, informing and educating you, the reader, on our journeys. The richness of the history of the biblical lands and the truth of the Bible has moved me to reach out in Discipleship Books Ministry, an ordinary person helping other ordinary people find their faith in Jesus Christ, our savior.

These books I have put on Amazon are the culmination of 20 years of research, discovery and worship in the Christian Church. In many ways, these books map my journey as a Christian coming to grips with the meaning of being a true follower of Christ, and how to be the best disciple of Jesus I can be.

I pray that these insights I reveal in my books can create the same positive enlightenment in you as they have in me.